Rejuvenate Your Spirit

21 Day Devotional Journal

By Talisa Lauray

Rejuvenate Your Spirit

21 Day Devotional Journal

By Talisa Lauray

For more information about Talisa Lauray, please access the author's website at the following Internet address: www.onetouchoflove.com

Table of Contents

Dedication

This book is for all the women struggling with feeling empty, lost, and alone. This is for all the women that don't know their purpose. This is for all the women struggling with depression and anxiety.

Introduction

As long as you live heartbreak will always exist, and there's nothing you can do about it. Heartbreak drains your spirit, sometimes to the point of feeling like there's no way out of the darkness. However, there is a way to be brought out of a dark place, by rejuvenating your spirit.

Heartbreak, in this book, doesn't limit itself to intimate relationships, but anything can break your spirit. Being financially unstable, natural disasters, sudden death of a loved one, and rejection are just a few examples of what can break you. When these things happen it's hard to see the light at the end of the tunnel. Sometimes you look at the end of the tunnel and see darkness, but if you keep walking toward the end, the light will appear and grow bigger. The bigger the light gets, the closer you are to getting out of the tunnel.

This book will help you get to the light spiritually so that you will not be stuck in the darkness of life. It will help you to get through the tunnel of anxiety, depression, or fear. It will also guide you to see yourself the way God sees you. This book will teach you God's will for your life so that you will never lose sight of the light again.

DAY 1: Spiritual Diet

On this twenty-one-day journey I hope you will learn more about God and yourself. The first day we will focus on cleansing. Physical cleanses are healthy for our bodies, to make sure the organs stay healthy, however, we must do the same thing spiritually.

Diets occur for many reasons, but the common factor is to lose weight. There might be a dress or suit for an occasion that is a couple of sizes too small; or the doctor may have given a bad report on health; whatever the reason, diets and cleansing are used to get rid of something physical. Eating is supposed to be a way to nurture our bodies as fuel, not to consume unnecessary junk food. The junk is there as a treat for enjoyment but not to depend on for fulfillment.

Just like the body, the spirit can get filled with too much junk. When our spirits get filled with junk, we get filled with thoughts that can clog our thinking. Our minds feel sluggish, overwhelmed, and confused. Anxiety and depression will try to take over our thoughts. Our mind isn't sound, and we lose track of our purpose. The Bible says, *"For God hath not given us the spirit of fear; but of power, and of love, and of a sound mind."* 2 Timothy 1:7

Let's define some things to get a better understanding of why a spiritual diet is important. Understanding what is attacking us brings deliverance.

1. Fear: "an emotion caused by belief that something bad is going to happen." [1]
2. Anxiety: "excessive feelings of fear, worry, and stress. Often results in muscle tension." [2]
3. Depression: "persistent feeling of sadness. The number 1 cause: stress." [3]
4. Belief: "an acceptance that something is true." [4]

We have the power to accept fear or faith, depending on what we believe in. We also have the power to control our thoughts, emotions, and our spirit, depending on what we believe in. There is a saying, "seeing is believing." A lot of Christians don't like this statement because it's stating belief only happens when something is seen. However, this statement is partially true.

There is a saying, "the eyes are the window to the soul." This statement is usually interpreted as "look into someone's eyes to see their soul" but the other interpretation is "what you see is what you become." In Matthew 6 Jesus gave the disciples lessons about different topics. One of the topics was money then after that Jesus talks about the eye. Matthew 6:22-23 says, *"The eye is the lamp of the body. If your eyes are healthy, your whole body will be full of light. But if your eyes are unhealthy, your whole body will be full of darkness. If then the light within you is darkness, how great is that darkness!"*

Reading or watching a lot of negative things will eventually take a toll on our spirits. Being surrounded by negative people will also take a toll on our spirits. This is why it is important to surround ourselves with positive affirmations and read the Bible. Eventually the surroundings will pierce our spirits, then we will believe what we always see. This is why it is important to cleanse our spirits.

After each day, there are questions and space for you to write your answers. This is important because this will help you to get to the root of what's causing the junk in your spirit. The negativity will then be pulled up and the only thing that will be left is what will be producing something great.

DAY 1: Spiritual Diet

Questions

1. Do I have a sound mind?
2. Do I worry too much?
3. Am I afraid about the future?
4. What do I worry about the most?

_____
_____
_____
_____
_____
_____
_____
_____
_____
_____
_____
_____
_____
_____
_____
_____
_____
_____
_____
_____
_____
_____
_____
_____
_____
_____

DAY 1: Spiritual Diet

Prayer

Dear Lord,

Thank You for the grace and mercy to be able to renew our spirits. We want to have a sound mind again. Please clean out our minds by exposing anything that isn't like you. Remove the spirit of fear, we don't accept it any more in our lives. We choose to trust you. Please fill us with your Holy Spirit. Speak to our hearts during this journey and beyond. In Jesus name, Amen.

_____

_____

_____

_____

_____

_____

_____

_____

_____

_____

_____

_____

_____

_____

_____

_____

_____

DAY 2: God's Desire

God wants us to have a full, prosperous life. He wants us to enjoy life. In John 10:10 Jesus stated, *"The thief does not come except to steal, and to kill, and to destroy. I have come that they may have life, and that they may have it more abundantly."*

Having life "more abundantly" doesn't mean trials and tribulations aren't going to happen. What does abundantly mean? It means plentiful and extreme. (5) Jesus came to give us more than extreme living, think about that for a second. That's an awesome thought. We are to just exist and do the best we can with our lives, then trust God to give us even more fulfillment. This life is not supposed to be filled with fear, depression, or worry. It's supposed to be filled with joy.

When I was younger things that came to mind when I heard the phrase "abundant life" is money and vacation. But now I understand that "abundant life" is peace and joy no matter what is happening around me. Abundant life is about what happens on the inside of our minds and spirits. It's what we believe in and how we react to situations. We learned in day one that we have the power to accept what we believe in. Today is about how to believe in God's desire, which is abundant living.

The best way to believe and achieve abundant life is keep God first. That's it, that's the answer. It sounds simple and it is simple to achieve. However, keeping

God first is a process. We are not to beat ourselves up if this doesn't happen all the time. Why? Because Jesus died for us to live a worry-free life which is also known as the abundant life.

I remember there was a "fad" going around for several years; it was called W.W.J.D., which stood for "What Would Jesus Do?" Some people didn't take it seriously, but some people did because it was an opportunity for Christians to share the love of God. For me, honestly, I would wear the bracelet at a young age and think about Jesus, but I would go back to being disobedient. I would still make my own decisions, which was not good, with the bracelet on. I would acknowledge the bracelet after I got in trouble and needed Jesus to get me out.

For some people, it genuinely changed their lives by reminding them to put God first in every decision. God's number one desire for us is we always think about W.W.J.D. He wants us to always put Him first in our decisions, thoughts, words and actions. The number one commandment is to put Him first. He is the only one, true living God and ALL He ask of us is to put Him first. This is where Jesus comes in because God knew the devil was going to try to snake his way into our lives to distract us from God's love. The devil's desire is to destroy us so that our belief (acceptance) is stronger in fear than in faith in God. When we operate more in fear, our focus is more on worrying then putting God first.

God sent Jesus to live on earth so that people would see for themselves because seeing is believing. Jesus died then rose again from death so that we would continue to believe in the resurrection. We would accept the belief of Jesus being God's son, died, rose on the third day and sitting at the right hand of God, our Father. When we genuinely believe this 24-7, we will have abundant life, we will be saved.

Romans 10:9 says, *"that if you confess with your mouth the Lord Jesus and believe in your heart that God has raised Him from the dead, you will be saved."*

My spirit is jumping up and down right now with excitement, I hope this excites you just as much. It's amazing to know that God is so powerful that all we must do is confess that we believe and then just be while believing. This means that when fear, doubt, and worry try to creep in our minds, we confess "No, I do not accept the spirit of fear, I accept that I believe in Jesus and He has given me abundant life. I believe that everything is going to be alright."

The confession isn't because we are not saved, the confession is to remind us that we are saved, and we have nothing to worry about. I have positive affirmations all over my house, but I also have scriptures as a reminder of God's faithfulness. I believe reciting our confession of faith in Jesus is abundantly more important than confessing how beautiful I am in the mirror. When I do affirmations in the mirror the first thing I say is, "I am a child of God." Then I talk about how beautiful I am. The statement, "I am a child of God" sums up I trust God, I believe in God, I love God, I listen to God, I'm obedient to God, He is my Father in heaven.

Luke 9:23 says, *"Then He said to them all, "If anyone desires to come after Me, let him deny himself, and take up his cross daily, and follow Me."*

Jesus is saying in this scripture put me first daily if this is your desire. My desire is to have God's desire for my life, and I assume that is the same for anyone embarking on this journey. Therefore, we must daily choose God's desires over our own. Which means if God says, "don't date that person, move to this city, don't watch this movie," then He is giving these directions for our protection so that we can have the abundant life.

Jesus left us with the Holy Spirit, His Spirit, to guide us to achieve God's desire. Jesus did that because He knew that we would need something to help us when we go our own way. The Holy Spirit is our helper, comfort, our GPS to get to the abundant life.

DAY 2: God's Desire

Questions

1. What decisions have you made recently that was wasn't God's answer?

2. What is the result of those decisions?

3. What decisions do you have to make now that you need God's help on?

_____
_____
_____
_____
_____
_____
_____
_____
_____
_____
_____
_____
_____
_____
_____
_____
_____
_____
_____

DAY 2: God's Desire

Prayer

Dear Lord,

Thank you for sending your son, Jesus. God, I confess with my heart and mouth. I believe (accept) that Jesus is God's son and God raised Him from the dead. I believe and accept God's desire of the abundant life Jesus died to give me. I pray that God will give me the strength to remember to put God first in every situation in my life. I pray God will give me eyes to see and the ears to hear my helper, the Holy Spirit, to guide me.

In Jesus name, Amen.

_____

_____

_____

_____

_____

_____

_____

_____

_____

_____

_____

_____

_____

_____

_____

DAY 3: The List

When bad things happen to us, it's hard to find the good in them. I know it sounds crazy but when I started to think of the things that happened to me that were bad, they truly worked out for my good. Today, I want you to focus on the things that you have been through that could have taken your life. The things that you survived, and you know that if it wasn't for God, you wouldn't be here today. Think about the bad times and find God in them. When we're going through something, God is always there.

I'll use my own life as an example. I went through a period of looking for love in the wrong places. I had a steady high school boyfriend, but the relationship wasn't good. I stayed in it because it was there and had approval from everyone on the outside, but I wasn't happy. I became codependent on him to the point that I followed him to his college of choice. I was trying to create the perfect scenario of high school sweethearts running off to college together, graduate, get married, have 2.5 children, and live happily ever after. I ended up heartbroken, but I still wanted to be with him, therefore, I did what I needed to do. I ended up pregnant at a young age of eighteen. The pregnancy grounded me by forcing me to totally depend on God. We ended up getting married then divorced after just two years. That time was very difficult for me. I didn't know who I was without being in a relationship. I attempted suicide because I thought without his love

I'm useless and no one is going to me love me. God's miraculous love saved me that day. I learned that God loves me, even when I don't love myself. God's love for me is enough for me to feel loved. However, I still continued to make bad decisions.

I ended up married to someone else a year later, not healed from the first marriage. This marriage was toxic and lasted over ten years. Out of these two failed marriages God gave me gifts. I have three amazing children, a blog, and books (many yet to be written).

When we meditate on the past mistakes that we made, God was always there. God can turn any situation around, even the situations we put ourselves in. God rescues us from everything. I can think of things I did financially, physically, and spiritually that God said, "NO," but I did it anyway. Then I would cry out to God to rescue me. God is such a good Father that He came every time. This is why we thank Him for His grace and mercy because God uses OUR bad choices for our good.

When God rescues, He also takes away the shame of our mistakes with His love. God removes our past so much that sometimes we forget what we went through. The statement, "I don't look like what I've been through" is true because God not only rescues but He also renews. He rejuvenates. God's love for us is just like a Father with ten children, for example. All the children make mistakes. When a new child is learning to walk falls happen, the child will start crying. The Father comes to rescue them. The comfort of the Father renews the spirit of the child so much that the child gets down and tries it again, this time without falling. Once the child gets the hang of walking the falls are forgotten. The only way the child remembers is if something reminds them or if there is a list of the falls.

Having a list of God's rescues is a reminder that God is our Father, and He has always been there to pick us up during the falls. I encourage everyone reading to make a list of the falls in your life God has rescued you from. You may not make it to the end without shouting for joy.

When I look back over my life and think about all the things God has done for me, I shout for joy because God is AMAZING! This is a great way to rejuvenate your spirit.

DAY 3: The List

Questions

Romans 8:28 "And we know that all things work together for good to those who love God, to those who are called according to His purpose."

Write down the bad things that happened to you, and then write down beside those the good things that has come out of it.

Three things will happen:

1. You will forgive yourself.

2. You will forgive others involved.

3. That situation will no longer have you bound because you will begin praise God for it therefore Satan can't use it against you anymore.

_____

_____

_____

_____

_____

_____

_____

_____

_____

_____

DAY 3: The List

Prayer

Dear Lord,

Thank you for being in control of everything. Thank you for delivering me from everything that was meant to hurt me. Thank you that everything that was meant for bad because it has worked out for my good. I pray that you will give me the opportunity to share these experiences as a testimony so others will be blessed. I praise you for your protection and love. Please continue to surround me with your grace and mercy.

In Jesus name. Amen.

_____

_____

_____

_____

_____

_____

_____

_____

_____

_____

_____

_____

_____

_____

DAY 4: Forgive Others and Yourself

You will need to refer to the list you made yesterday for today. Okay, let's break down this word in its syllables: for-give-ness.

1. For- is used as a function to indicate purpose. (7)
2. Give - a transfer of authority from one person to the other. (8)
3. Ness - is state; condition; quality; degree. (9)

Forgiveness is the state of purpose to transfer authority. When you forgive someone, you take back the authority over that hurt, the pain, and the trauma it caused in your life. Your decisions will no longer be based on hurt but based on forgiveness. For example, after an abusive relationship with a man, whether its verbal or physical, a woman is going to have heartache. This type of heartache is called baggage because it's carried with her into future relationships. She might start to view every man as the one that hurt her until she forgives him wholeheartedly. It will be hard for her to trust and receive love from other men without forgiveness. This hurt woman will often respond in anger instead of love. She could possibly be defensive because of the wall she has up, and this is going to make it difficult to be submissive to her future husband. The woman then is labeled as bitter or angry, but she is just walking in unforgiveness because of the baggage she carries. She must forgive in order to receive.

Many of us are walking in unforgiveness carrying around baggage. This baggage can be toward the people that hurt us or toward ourselves. We carry hurt and disappointment toward ourselves for some of the decisions we made in the past that were life changing. Forgiveness toward ourselves will cause us to treat ourselves with kindness as well as bring more confidence and remove shame. It's hard to self-love when it feels like you don't deserve love. Believe you deserve love because you do.

Today is the day to stop beating yourself up over the past mistakes you've made. You are holding yourself back because of unforgiveness. God is ready to reveal the purpose He has for you. His desire is to give you an abundant life. However, the unforgiveness for yourself is causing you to not be able to receive from God. Mark 11:25 says, *"And whenever you stand praying, if you have anything against anyone, forgive him, that your Father in heaven may also forgive you your trespasses."*

Forgive yourself. Forgive others. God will forgive you and pour out blessings.

DAY 4: Forgive Others and Yourself

Questions

Use the list from yesterday as a guide to meditate on these things and say to each item on the list, "I forgive you." Let God clean your heart of unforgiveness. Do this in silence with no distractions so you can really hear from Him.

_____

_____

_____

_____

_____

_____

_____

_____

_____

_____

_____

_____

_____

_____

_____

_____

_____

_____

_____

_____

_____

_____

DAY 4: Forgive Others and Yourself

Prayer

Dear Lord,

Thank you for forgiving me for my sins. Please God, allow me to walk in forgiveness toward myself, and anyone that has hurt me. I don't want to be angry anymore. I don't want to walk around carrying bags of shame and guilt. These bags are heavy and I'm tired of carrying them. I want to walk toward my purpose and receive what You have for me. Fill me with your Holy Spirit so that when my forgiveness is tested, I will stand firm in my decision to forgive. Thank you, Jesus.

In Jesus name, Amen.

_____
_____
_____
_____
_____
_____
_____
_____
_____
_____
_____
_____

DAY 5: Be Gentle Toward Others and Yourself

There are many people that don't like to describe themselves as gentle or meek because they think it makes them weak. Being gentle or meek actually makes them stronger. It doesn't mean they will let people run over them but the initial response to a situation shouldn't always be offensiveness. The response to situations should be gentleness, which is a characteristic of the Holy Spirit.

Being gentle is important because it represents God. When we receive the Holy Spirit, our character should change to reflect it. Galatians 5:22-23 says, *"But the fruit of the Spirit is love, joy, peace, longsuffering, kindness, goodness, faithfulness, gentleness, self-control. Against such there is no law."*

Having an offensive, tough spirit all the time stirs up division and destroys. We have seen this a lot in the media lately. People are so quick to point out someone's flaws and argue without first being gentle. I believe if we walked in the spirit of gentleness, it would prevent half of the stuff that goes on in the world. There have been a couple of news reports where people lost their lives because of road rage. Road rage? Come on! How is life threatened in a car? If those people had the spirit of gentleness the person would still be alive, and the killer wouldn't be in jail. Those lives are destroyed. Remember who is the king of destroying lives? The devil. Who is the Prince of Peace? Jesus. Be gentle. Don't be a destroyer.

Mathew 5:5 says, *"Blessed are those who are meek, for they will inherit the earth."*

If a person is angry toward you, still walk in gentleness. I know this is easier said than done. Eventually if the gentleness is strong enough, it will rub off on the person. It's hard to hear a person that is yelling because the person listening isn't focused on what is being said but how it is being said.

When my daughter was a baby, I used to read to her my college books. I had to study and entertain my child at the same time because she wanted quality time with me. I would read my college book in a tone that was gentle so that she wouldn't cry. I used a happy, soft voice so I could focus on learning while taking care of my daughter. She didn't care what I was reading but my spirit was gentle while I was reading to keep her from crying. Think about this when dealing with adults also. Being gentle makes a huge difference when dealing with angry people. Of course, if you're in physical danger then that's different.

Don't just be gentle with others, be gentle with yourself. Some of us look back over our lives and are truly grateful for everything God brought them through. The opposite of this is being hard on ourselves for not being where we want to be in life. Everyone makes mistakes. There is no perfect person on earth. Be gentle with yourself.

God has you where He wants you. Don't beat yourself up mentally because you are not where you want to be. Turn the regret to thankfulness by thanking God you could be in a worse place. Honestly, we all could be worse off than where we are in life now. Trust that God has a plan to prosper you and seek Him.

DAY 5: Be Gentle Toward Others and Yourself

Questions

Write areas in your life where you can improve on gentleness, whether it's toward people at work or even your own family.

_____

_____

_____

_____

_____

_____

_____

_____

_____

_____

_____

_____

_____

_____

_____

_____

_____

_____

_____

_____

_____

_____

_____

DAY 5: Be Gentle Toward Others and Yourself

Prayer

Dear Lord,

Thank you for allowing me to see another day. Lord please forgive me for not walking in the spirit of gentleness. Please help me to be gentle in these areas that I listed. I need help because I want to be an example of peace and not a destroyer. Help me to be gentle with myself. Remove the spirit of defensiveness from my heart and put in gentleness.

In Jesus name. Amen.

_____

_____

_____

_____

_____

_____

_____

_____

_____

_____

_____

_____

_____

_____

_____

_____

_____

DAY 6: Be Patient Toward Others and Yourself

In this day and time, patience is something that many of us struggle with, especially when we're going through something. Maybe if we understand patience more then we will know how important it is. The definition of patience is "bearing pain or trials calmly or without complaint." (10) Being patient is deeper than just waiting, it's a description of how to wait.

We are supposed to be remaining calm in any situation because we know God is in control. We should wait patiently while seeking God for guidance on what to do next. We should keep our faith in God while waiting patiently.

"Jesus wept," John 11:35 is a very popular scripture because it's the shortest scripture that we memorized at Vacation Bible School as kids. The story behind this scripture starts in verse 1 of chapter 11 when Jesus first heard that Lazarus was sick. Jesus said that God is going to get the glory out of his sickness therefore Jesus stayed where He was two more days instead of rushing to heal Lazarus. Jesus was calm without complaint. Jesus knew that Lazarus was going to live. The sisters that sent for Jesus thought that He was talking about living in heaven. They didn't believe that Jesus could bring him back to life on earth. The women were crying with sorrow because they felt like if Jesus had come sooner Lazarus wouldn't have died. When Jesus saw Lazarus laying in the tomb and the sisters were crying,

this is when Jesus wept. Jesus was heartbroken because of their unbelief. He wasn't crying because he missed Lazarus, he was crying because the sisters were so hurt that Jesus didn't come on time. The next thing Jesus did was tell Lazarus to get up. Many commentaries state Jesus felt their sorrow, which is true, but Jesus was also trying to convince them He was about to raise Lazarus again. I believe Jesus does feel our sorrows, and Jesus wept because of their unbelief. He didn't want them to be sad and worried, He wanted them to have faith that Lazarus wasn't really dead on earth from sickness.

The miracle of Jesus raising Lazarus from the dead increased the faith of His believers even more. Jesus healed many from sickness, but from the dead, it seemed impossible. Sometimes the wait isn't about us but it's about God getting more glory out of our lives. The miracle God does in our lives will be an example to many and will cause them to believe more in Jesus when we tell our testimony.

Yesterday we talked about being gentle, gentle and patience go hand in hand. Patience is the first characteristic to describe love. Love covers all. When you are patient, you love. The opposite of patient is anxiousness. A specific example is a teenager who has a snappy attitude. The impatient response is to snap back and use your age as an authority. The teenager will feel attacked and will snap back, then a fight has broken out. No one in this scenario is helped but the situation is made worse.

The patient response is to get to the bottom of the snappy attitude in a gentle way. The teenager could be having issues at home, or it might just be their character and deliverance is needed. Either way, being patient and gentle with someone can change their life for the better. As a result of being patient, you help the teenager instead of adding more pain to their wounds.

2 Timothy 2:24-25 says, *"And a servant of the Lord must not quarrel but be gentle to all, able to teach, patient in humility correcting those who are in opposition with God."*

Be patient with yourself. You will be successful. You will overcome everything that is trying to attack you. Life is a process. Be gentle with yourself. Seek God while being patient and gentle with yourself. He will get you through anything.

DAY 6: Be Patient Toward Others and Yourself

Questions

1. Why is it important to be patient?

2. What areas in your life can you be more patient in?

3. How can you be more patient with yourself?

_____

_____

_____

_____

_____

_____

_____

_____

_____

_____

_____

_____

_____

_____

_____

_____

_____

_____

_____

_____

_____

_____

_____

DAY 6: Be Patient Toward Others and Yourself

Prayer

Dear Lord,

Thank you for all you've done for me. Please forgive me for being impatient with people. Lord, I pray that when opportunities come up for me to be patient, your Holy Spirit will control me and allow me to be patient. I want to walk in love and not hurt people. Please help me to be patient with myself. I don't always make the wisest decisions. I must be patient so that I will be successful. I must be patient with You too Lord. Thank You, Jesus, for your patience with me.

In Jesus name. Amen.

_____

_____

_____

_____

_____

_____

_____

_____

_____

_____

_____

_____

_____

DAY 7: Be Loving Toward Yourself

Being gentle and patient with yourself leads us to love yourself. Don't feel guilty for loving yourself, especially if you have children. Again, don't feel guilty for loving yourself.

When someone asks you to pick them up to take them somewhere, the first thing that comes to mind is how much gas is in the car. It's impossible to give someone a ride if you don't have enough gas in your car first. If you run out of gas, you'll both be walking. Gas is love in this analogy.

It's important to make sure that we have enough love for ourselves to overflow to others. Love for us includes physically, emotionally, spiritually and mentally taking care of ourselves. It's tough being mentally exhausted from stress at work, then having to go home and care for a family. Taking a few minutes to sit in the car in the driveway to gather ourselves sometimes is necessary to refuel our minds with love to give to our families. Walking into the house after a stressful day without refilling ourselves with love might result in unexplained impatience when dealing with others. The impatience might result in an argument that could've been prevented if we filled ourselves up with love first.

Loving ourselves is in the Bible. Matthew 22:39 says, *"And the second is like it: 'You shall love your neighbor as yourself.'"* The disciples asked Jesus, "What is the greatest commandment?" The first one is love God. The second commandment of all the commandments is love your neighbor as yourself. Jesus is saying love yourself and your neighbor equally. If we don't love ourselves, does that mean we don't love others? It doesn't mean that you don't love others, but not loving ourselves makes it hard to love others.

I will use myself as an example. One of the ways I loved me when I was broken is with therapy. The most beneficial tool I learned in therapy is that we all have love tanks. The love tank is what makes us feel loved. These tanks get empty, just like a gas tank, when we use up all of the love. We feel drained because we have poured so much out before we are able to refill. The tanks don't just get empty from what we pour out, they also get empty from what we let in, like putting bad gas in a car.

Make sure whatever you choose to love yourself still brings glory to God. Don't do things that are harmful to yourself or will make your situation worse. Loving yourself should be helpful to you in all areas. An example of causing more harm is maxing out a credit card for retail therapy.

Today, journal on ways to fill your own love tank. You shouldn't depend on anyone else to fill it for you, even if you are married. Love yourself to the point that your tank is never empty. Write down stress relievers that you can do for yourself that makes you feel good about yourself.

DAY 7: Be Loving Toward Yourself

Questions

1. Write down how you fill your love tank.

_____
_____
_____
_____
_____
_____
_____
_____
_____
_____
_____
_____
_____
_____
_____
_____
_____
_____
_____
_____
_____
_____
_____
_____
_____
_____
_____
_____
_____
_____

DAY 7: Be Loving Toward Yourself

Prayer

Dear Lord,

Thank you so much for always loving me when I didn't love myself. Thank you for loving my friends and family. Please keep me filled up with your love so that I can love everyone else with the overflow that you have put in me. Please give me the strength to not depend on anyone to fill my tank. I want you to always fill my love tank. Give me wisdom to know the right way to love myself.

In Jesus name, Amen.

_____

_____

_____

_____

_____

_____

_____

_____

_____

_____

_____

_____

_____

_____

DAY 8: Be Loving Toward Others

Love is the greatest and most powerful gift from the Holy Spirit. Without love none of us would be here. It's not just the greatest gift but it's also the number one commandment.

"And above all things have fervent love for one another, for "love will cover a multitude of sins." 1 Peter 4:8

What does this mean? 1 Corinthians 13:4-6 says,

"Love suffers long and is kind; love does not envy; love does not parade itself, is not [b]puffed up; does not behave rudely, does not seek its own, is not provoked, [c]thinks no evil; does not rejoice in iniquity, but rejoices in the truth; bears all things, believes all things, hopes all things, endures all things."

Culture has created different views on love that don't line up with the Bible. Cancel culture is an example of something that is the opposite of love. Canceling someone because they do something wrong is not an act of love, instead covering them by showing them grace is love.

Don't close the book. I think I lost half of the culture by that statement, but it's in the Bible. When you talk to someone with love instead of condemning, it makes a huge difference in how they respond. When someone has done something wrong, pointing out their flaws shouldn't cause them to feel guilt, but cause them to feel forgiven. We must lead people to the cross and not push them away with condemnation. This is how and why love is so important.

I can think of a time in my life when I felt condemned. I was eighteen years old and pregnant. I felt so ashamed of myself already, then someone else came along to make me feel worse. I was so depressed I was sick. I lost weight in my first three months of being pregnant. It wasn't just morning sickness, but I lost my joy. I finally told my mom I was pregnant, and she was upset. Then after a few moments of being upset, she prayed with me. I found a new respect for my mom that day. She immediately had love toward me. Her act of love changed my life because I knew everything was going to be okay. Her love gave me the strength I needed to enjoy the gift of having a baby.

Love changes things and it is so powerful. Love is a feeling we all know, but it has to be more to love, right? The reason I ask this is because feeling applies to something you can feel. Love isn't something you do just when you feel like it; it's something you become. We describe the devil as evil and mean. How do we describe God? God is love. It is His being. It's His superpower. When we demonstrate love, we show others God.

God says in His word that if we do not show others love than we don't know Him. This is a hard truth to swallow because we have all had moments when we didn't act in love. Talking about someone behind their back isn't love. Manipulative and narcissism behavior isn't love. Being angry and unforgiving isn't love. These examples are things God wouldn't do therefore neither should we. We must demonstrate and become love so that people know whom we belong to, Jesus. I encourage you all to not just desire to be in love but to become love.

Becoming love will rejuvenate your spirit. You will start to find joy in the bad things around you. Love will give you an optimistic perspective on everything.

DAY 8: Be Loving Toward Others

Questions

1. Read 1 Corinthians 13
2. Why is love important?
3. What is love?
4. How can you demonstrate love to others?

_____

_____

_____

_____

_____

_____

_____

_____

_____

_____

_____

_____

_____

_____

_____

_____

_____

_____

_____

_____

_____

_____

DAY 8: Be Loving Toward Others

Prayer

Dear Lord,

Thank you for giving me the greatest gift of love. Thank you for loving me. Help me to love others unconditionally, including my enemies. Help me to receive love from you and other people. Help me to walk in forgiveness and discernment also. Thank you that your love covers all of my wrongs.

In Jesus name. Amen.

_____

_____

_____

_____

_____

_____

_____

_____

_____

_____

_____

_____

_____

_____

DAY 9: God's Gift

There are several instances in the Old Testament of the Bible where people were filled with God's Spirit. One example is Micah who was chosen by God to speak to the people of Judah and Israel about their rebellion. He speaks against false prophets and says they do not know God. Micah 3:8 states, *"He is filled with the power of God."*

The Holy Spirit is there to lead us, guide us, and to give us wisdom. People that don't believe call it instincts, gut feeling, or heart but the truth is God's spirit speaks to everyone. God loves everyone and He left is Spirit to everyone. I know I said everyone more than once. I want everyone to understand that non-believers hear the Holy Spirit, but they don't believe so they don't know what it is that is protecting them. John 14:17 says, *"the Spirit of truth, whom the world cannot receive, because it neither sees Him nor knows Him; but you know Him, for He dwells with you and will be in you."*

The closer we get to God the stronger the Holy Spirit's presence is in our lives. When we receive and believe Jesus as our Lord and Savior, we are then filled with the Holy Spirit. Acts 4:31 *"And when they had prayed, the place where they were assembled together was shaken; and they were all filled with the Holy*

Spirit, and they spoke the word of God with boldness."

God is calling but only those calling Him back will be filled. For example, the dad with ten children calls all of them to come to him because he must give them something that's going to change their life. Only five out of the ten children go to receive it. The five children received the blessing, but the dad still loves all the children. He still cooks for all of them but only the five that were obedient were given something life changing to help them.

In Romans 8:6 it states, *"the mind-set of the flesh is death, but the mind-set of the Spirit is life and peace."*

If something on our mind doesn't give us life and peace, it's not from God. The result or the fruit of the instructions should bring peace, love, joy, comfort and life. The result of the flesh or the devil is destruction.

We must keep the voice that is giving us peace louder than the voice that wants to destroy us. How? By continuously filling our spirits with the Word and spending time in prayer. If we keep eating sugar all the time, eventually we are going to gain weight and possibly diabetes. The same thing happens to our spirit; if we keep filling our spirits with a bunch of negativities then it's going to fill our minds up with the wrong voice.

Anxiety, worry, and depression will enter our minds through fear.

It's hard to hear more than one person talk at a time. Teachers have a classroom of at least thirty students. If every student spoke up all at it once, it creates a lot of confusion. The child with the right answer cannot be heard because everyone else is talking over that child. This is why the teacher ask the children to raise their hand when they know the answer. This will allow the correct answer to be heard while all the other children, distractions, are quiet.

We must do the same thing which is quieting the distractions with the Word of God in order to hear the Holy Spirit. We must silence the distractions so that the right answer, the Holy Spirit, can be heard.

DAY 9: God's Gift

Questions

1. What is another name for the Holy Spirit?
2. Which voice has been louder to you, God's or your own?
3. How can you make the voice of the Spirit louder in your life?

_____
_____
_____
_____
_____
_____
_____
_____
_____
_____
_____
_____
_____
_____
_____
_____
_____
_____
_____
_____

DAY 9: God's Gift

Prayer

Dear Lord,

I thank you so much for giving me your Holy Spirit. Please help me to hear your voice and obey it. I want the Holy Spirit to guide, comfort and give me peace. I want the Holy Spirit to give me your wisdom and understanding. Make it clear to me your voice so that I will be obedient to it. Reveal to me what distractions I need to remove so that your voice is loudest in my life.

In Jesus name, Amen.

_____

_____

_____

_____

_____

_____

_____

_____

_____

_____

_____

_____

_____

_____

DAY 10: Desire Wisdom

I've heard several times that "we don't take with us what we learn in school." What we do take is the work ethic and discipline to do the work. School is a ton of memorizing. What we do take with us is the wisdom to figure things out. For example, you never forget the basics of math because they are embedded in our minds. The basics are multiplication, subtraction, division, and addition. We used the basics for everyday living therefore we have knowledge and wisdom of the basics of math.

Knowledge and Wisdom are two different things. What is wisdom? Wisdom is applying knowledge in an insightful way. (12) Being wise is showing the knowledge and experience. This is why people say that statement of not taking everything with us we learned in school. Everything we learn isn't wisdom because we can't use it. Some stuff is just knowledge.

What should we do with the knowledge we are going to learn along this journey, we should use wisdom and apply it to our lives. Our desire from God should be to get more knowledge about His purpose for our lives, knowledge about God Himself, knowledge about ourselves and then ask God for wisdom. Our desire should also be to understand God and the Bible.

Everything will not be revealed. The Bible is known to be one of the most controversial books on earth because for some readers it has too many inconsistencies in it. I don't fully understand everything in the Bible either, and honestly, I believe no one does. I believe God created it that way so that believers will never stop seeking understanding. Only God is all knowing and if man were to fully understand everything about God, He wouldn't be God.

Even Jesus's disciples didn't understand everything. They basically lived with Jesus and didn't have all their questions answered. This is why faith and trust in God are important. This is also why it's important to have a relationship with God. Everyone's relationship with God is different. It's just a dad that has ten children, each child's relationship is different with the same dad because of their different personalities. This is why it's important for us, as children of God, not to judge one another but walk in love. God loves all of us. We are all different and our relationship with God is different. One thing remains the same, God.

This is a short day because I want you all to read Proverbs Chapters 1-3. These three chapters discuss what wisdom is and why it is important.

DAY 10: Desire Wisdom

Questions

1. What is true wisdom?
2. What does God do for those who seek His wisdom?
3. What makes a person happy?

_____

_____

_____

_____

_____

_____

_____

_____

_____

_____

_____

_____

_____

_____

_____

_____

_____

_____

_____

_____

_____

DAY 10: Desire Wisdom

Prayer

Dear Lord,

Thank you so much for your Word. I thank you for giving me the ability to receive knowledge of you through the Bible. I thank you for allowing me to have a relationship with you. I pray that you will give me wisdom as I empty out all the junk from my spirit. I pray that as I grow closer to you, wisdom grows in me so that your light will shine through me.

In Jesus name. Amen.

_____

_____

_____

_____

_____

_____

_____

_____

_____

_____

_____

_____

_____

_____

DAY 11: Know God as a Father

Many people say that it is hard to see God as father when it seems like so many bad things keep happening to them. However, God is our father. He loves us more than we love our children. He loves us more than our parents. Knowing God as father teaches us who we are.

In modern culture, it's tradition we get our last name from our fathers because the man is known to be the leader of the family. The family takes on the man's identity. Families were known because of what the man of the house did as an occupation. In the same way when we confess we are a child of God, we take on His identity. God is our Father in heaven.

As a parent, we love our children; we give them what we have financially, spiritually and mentally. We keep them from what we think is going to harm them and we punish them when they are disobedient because we don't want our kids to get hurt. We want to teach our kids the right way. We work hard so they can inherit something great. God treats us the same way. He wants the best for us, but He isn't going to give us more than we can bear. God isn't going to give us a ton of money if it's going to cause harm and keep us from seeking Him.

God isn't going to let us keep doing whatever we want to do without showing us that's not the way. I have to monitor my son's time on his video game, especially when school is in session. If my son had his way, he would stay up until two o'clock in the morning playing the game, then sleep at school. However. I help him learn that this isn't right by taking his game system away during the week. If my son had more self-control, I would let him keep his gaming system. By taking my son's game system away, I'm helping him with his weakness. My son has a choice, he can find another way to not do well in school. If he decides this, he is disobeying me and will not reap the benefits of obedience. His life will be harder because he didn't do what I told him to do.

Proverbs 13 describes what happens when disobedience is done. There is a consequence to every choice that we make, especially as children of God. Yes, we have grace and mercy, but obedience to our Father in heaven will save us a lot heartache. Obedience will pull us out of the heartache that we are currently in.

There's nothing on earth that my own biological children can do that will cause me to stop loving them and being there for them when they call on me. I might punish them, give them a lecture, tell them no sometimes, but that doesn't change my love for them because they are my children.

I want you to know that you haven't done anything to stop God from loving you. It's not too late to repent and turn back to God, the Father. I guarantee that He is waiting there for you with open arms. God wants to love us like a father.

The following Bible verses describe who we are as children of God.

1. **You are wonderfully made.** *"I will praise You, for I am fearfully and wonderfully made; marvelous are Your works, and that my soul knows very well."* Psalm 139:14

2. **You are more than a conqueror.** *"Yet in all these things we are more than conquerors through Him who loved us."* Romans 8:37

3. **You can do anything that's God's will.** *"I can do all things through [a]Christ who strengthens me."* Philippians 4:13

4. **You are a producer.** *"I am the vine; you are the branches. He who abides in Me, and I in him, bears much fruit; for without Me you can do nothing."* John 15:5

5. **You are created to do good.** *"For we are His workmanship, created in Christ Jesus for good works, which God prepared beforehand that we should walk in them."* Ephesians 2:10

6. **You are a leader and blessed.** *"And the LORD will make you the head and not the tail; you shall be above only, and not be beneath, if you heed the commandments of the LORD your God, which I command you*

today, and are careful to observe them." Deuteronomy 28:13

7. **You are a peacemaker.** *"Blessed are the peacemakers; for they shall be called the children of God."* Matthew 5:9

DAY 11: Know God as a Father

Questions

Luke 15:11-32 is the parable of the prodigal son. Please look at this story.

1. Why did the son leave?
2. Why did the son want to go back home?
3. What was the father's reaction to his return?

_____

_____

_____

_____

_____

_____

_____

_____

_____

_____

_____

_____

_____

_____

DAY 11: Know God as a Father

Prayer

Dear Lord,

Thank you for being my heavenly Father. I receive your love as a fatherly love. I thank you for loving me and keeping me on the right path just like any parent would. I pray that I will continue to see you as Father.

In Jesus name. Amen.

_____
_____
_____
_____
_____
_____
_____
_____
_____
_____
_____
_____
_____
_____
_____
_____
_____

DAY 12: You're Gifted

Everyone has unique spiritual gifts from God. Jesus tells us in John 14, we can do the same works He did on earth. He gives us the power to do this through spiritual gifts. We all have the Holy Spirit, but we all have specific gifts that stand out more than the others. Remember we are a family. The Bible describes it as being a part of the body of Christ. Just like our physical bodies, each part has a different function, but it works together. When something is out of whack in our bodies, we are made aware because of pain. It's the same thing in the body of Christ when something is out of whack then it doesn't function like it's supposed to. This is why it is important that we know our spiritual gifts and how to use them.

1 Corinthians 2:4-7 says, *"There are diversities of gifts, but the same Spirit. 5 There are differences of ministries, but the same Lord. 6 And there are diversities of activities, but it is the same God who works all in all. 7 But the manifestation of the Spirit is given to each one for the profit of all:"*

A spiritual gift is something that is done to help people spiritually. Spiritual gifts can and are supposed to be used in our everyday lives, not just on Sunday for church. The gifts become part of our character as described in Galatians 5. The gifts help us to produce the "fruit" that Jesus talks about in John 15:5. The fruit isn't about money or children, but about helping others spiritually. Fruit is healthy for our physical bodies, but God wants us to produce something healthy spiritually too.

There are several places in the Bible that describe spiritual gifts. Some of the gifts describe the roles that are done in the church, while others describe roles outside of the church. The things outside of the church are what we can do if we are not called to be an apostle, prophet, evangelist, shepherd, or teacher as described in Ephesians 4:11-16. These describe the actual titles people have in the church. There are some people that have these gifts but don't have the title in the church. Side note: Just because we don't have the official title in the church doesn't mean we aren't these things.

I believe we are all called to tell others about God. As children of God, we are to tell others about how good our Father is. There is something about a child of God that carries a light that people are attracted to. When we receive the Holy Spirit, we receive the gift to spread the gospel. This is done however God leads you to do it. Many people have more than one path to share God with others. Some gifts are stronger and performed more naturally than other gifts.

I'll use myself for example, I'm a writer but I know eventually I'm going to start speaking more. Words come easier for me when I write because I'm not nervous. When I get up in front of people, I become nervous, and I don't always articulate clearly. Writing comes naturally to me, and I love it; speaking is something that I can do, but I must work hard to do it correctly. The way to find your spiritual gift is by seeking God first and then studying. Learn your passion. Your passion will turn into an avenue for you to use your spiritual gifts.

Your passion doesn't necessarily have to be with words. You might be a natural at being organized. I know a lot of people that are gifted in owning and running a successful business. They use those businesses to help people. Seeking God and getting to know God as Father are the first steps to discover spiritual gifts. Learning your gifts will help keep your spirit rejuvenated because they will give you purpose.

DAY 12: You're Gifted

Questions

Read 1 Corinthians 12 for more on spiritual gifts.

1. Do you enjoy helping others?
2. Do you enjoy teaching?
3. What are you passionate about?
4. Do you find yourself giving advice to others often?
5. What is the one thing you would do even if no one paid you?

_____

_____

_____

_____

_____

_____

_____

_____

_____

_____

_____

_____

_____

_____

_____

_____

_____

_____

_____

DAY 12: You're Gifted

Prayer

Dear Lord,

Thank you for blessing me with spiritual gifts. I ask that you will reveal the gifts you have given to me so that I can be effective and know my purpose. I want to do the works that you did so that others will know about you. I want you to get the glory God.

In Jesus name. Amen

_____

_____

_____

_____

_____

_____

_____

_____

_____

_____

_____

_____

_____

_____

_____

_____

_____

_____

_____

DAY 13: God Heals Broken Hearts

Healing is usually referenced to only be for our physical bodies but it's also for our broken hearts. Our emotions and mental health can be healed. God's desire is that we are whole.

Healing our broken emotions is a process. The process must start with the will to want to be healed. There are some people that don't realize they are broken emotionally until they feel so heavy, they are ready to take their own life. There are others that want to stay broken because they want to choose the path they want instead of changing.

Healing from a broken heart usually requires a lot of looking deep inside ourselves to see why the broken heart happened. I will use myself for example, I jumped into a marriage in my early twenties even though God told me not to take that leap. I went to therapy to help me heal and learned that my desire to want to be loved stems from some childhood hurt. I was able to uproot that stem so that I can heal and never make that mistake again. A lot of people don't want to do the work it takes to uproot the stems that caused them to make bad decisions.

Every broken heart doesn't come from bad choices made, sometimes it's just life. Losing a loved one to death causes a broken heart. Losing a job or the rising cost of living is causing a lot of stress and broken hearts these days.

The good news is God is a healer of the broken heart, no matter the cause.

Psalms 34:18 says, *"The LORD is close to the brokenhearted and saves those who are crushed in spirit."*

Psalms 147:3 says, *"He heals the brokenhearted and binds up their wounds."*

How does God heal our broken hearts? We must go to Him in prayer, spend time reading our Bible, investing in more books like this, to guide us on our journeys. Everything we want in life we must go and get. If we want food we have to go to the store or to the restaurant. If we want money to buy the food we have to make money. In order to make more money we have to go to classes to learn how to do something. If we want clothes we have to go shopping at the mall.

In Matthew 11:28-30 Jesus says, *"Come to me, all you who are weary and burdened, and I will give you rest. Take my yoke upon you and learn from me, for I am gentle and humble in heart, and you will find rest for your souls. For my yoke is easy and my burden is light."*

Jesus is saying I will take all of your burdens and give you rest, but you have to come to me to get it. The amazing part about this is it's free! We don't have to use gas to go get it. We don't have to work long hours to get this healing in our emotions. All we have to do is believe, trust, and, pray. Pray as many times as you need to. Pray without ceasing to feel the peace and love of God surround you.

Sometimes we have to lay on our faces, close out the world, and talk to God. Remember, talking to God also includes listening. The Holy Spirit will guide you. He will speak to the broken part of your emotions and start to heal you.

DAY 13: God Heals Broken Hearts

Questions

1. What has broken your heart?
2. Is there anything from childhood you need healing?
3. What steps are you going to take to heal?

_____

_____

_____

_____

_____

_____

_____

_____

_____

_____

_____

_____

_____

_____

_____

_____

_____

_____

_____

_____

_____

DAY 13: God Heals Broken Hearts

Prayer

Dear Lord,

Thank you for your will to heal broken hearts. Thank you for your Holy Spirit. I'm coming to you today because I have some brokenness in my life that need healing. Your Word says to come to you, so here I am. Please make me whole and help me to understand how I became broken. If there is something from my childhood that is keeping me emotionally broken, please reveal it and heal it.

In Jesus name. Amen.

_____

_____

_____

_____

_____

_____

_____

_____

_____

_____

_____

_____

_____

DAY 14: Seek God

There are many times in our lives when it feels like God is quiet. The silence leaves us wondering where God is in our situation. God is always with us. I'm a living testimony of God being there in my darkest hour of loneliness, broke, and brokenness. The silence and darkness are when we should seek God with more determination.

There are many times in our lives when everything is going perfect. All the bills are paid, extra money in the savings and checking accounts, the family is healthy, kids are making good grades, and the neighbor's dog isn't irritating. This is when we should seek God wholeheartedly.

Seek God in the good times and the bad times. Seeking God is like living a healthy lifestyle spiritually. Physical healthy lifestyles consist of eating a balanced diet and exercising regularly. A balance diet usually involves making sure to eat more vegetables and lean protein more than salty, sweet foods. If too much salty and sweet foods are eaten, the calorie count will go up and weight will be gained.

Weight gain can happen spiritually. We can gain the weight of the world on our shoulders when negative thoughts are more consumed than positive thoughts. Dwelling on the lack of money can be stressful, instead pray for wisdom to make extra money. Pray for the strength and health to carry out the plan to make more money.

Seeking God while everything is going well compares to maintaining the weight loss after a strict diet and exercise. In order to keep the weight off, consistent exercise and eating healthy have to be done. In order to keep the weight of the world off your shoulders, consistent praying and reading the Bible has to be done.

Jesus overcame the world when He defeated death. When we believe in Him, we overcome the world too. There are two scriptures in the Bible that explain this:

1. John 16: 33 says, *"These things I have spoken to you, that in Me you may have peace. In the world you will have tribulation; but be of good cheer, I have overcome the world."*
2. 1 John 5:4 says, *"For whatever is born of God overcomes the world. And this is the victory that has overcome the world—our faith."*

No worry or anxiety should enter our minds if we keep feeding our faith. We eat every day physically; we must eat every day spiritually.

In the Bible there's a woman with a health issue. She had it for at least twelve years trying to find solutions but there was none to be found. One day she heard Jesus was coming through town. She knew that she had to take action. She didn't sit around and wait for Jesus to come to her, she went to Him.

When she arrived, there was a crowd of people, but she didn't let that stop her. She believed that she had to get to Jesus for her healing. She had to press her way through the crowd to touch Him. She didn't touch his skin, but the hem of His clothes.

Sometimes we have to press our way through the crowd of negative thoughts as well as the crowd of everything going wrong in our life to get to Jesus. Once we receive a touch from Him, we will be changed for the better.

If seeking God doesn't give the immediate results you're searching for, don't stop seeking Him. You have to keep pressing in to Him. God promises several times in the Bible that He will be found by those that seek Him.

DAY 14: Seek God

Questions

1. What has God said to you recently in a way you didn't expect?
2. How did He speak to you?
3. How has He blessed you in a way you didn't expect?
4. Have you sought God? If so, what is He telling you to do?

_____

_____

_____

_____

_____

_____

_____

_____

_____

_____

_____

_____

_____

_____

_____

_____

_____

_____

_____

_____

DAY 14: Seek God

Prayer

Dear Lord,

Please forgive me for not being patient with you regarding my situation. I am ready to seek you for the answer. Please fill me with your Holy Spirit so that I will obey your answer. Give me the mind set to seek you as part of my lifestyle. Thank you, Lord, for Your love and being with me.

In Jesus name. Amen.

_____
_____
_____
_____
_____
_____
_____
_____
_____
_____
_____
_____
_____
_____
_____
_____
_____

DAY 15: Planted

The process of healing might require isolation. No one likes being alone but to be made whole, it might be necessary. It's hard to be around people while growing because they might be part of what is holding us back from wholeness. Sometimes the isolation is the only way God can plant us.

God wants to establish us with roots in Him that won't break. I recently separated and planted mint in two different pots so I could have more. The process reminded me of what God has to do with us sometimes so we can grow bigger. In order for my mint to grow, I had to separate some of them. First, I had to uproot them from where they were planted. Then I separated the roots, I dug a hole in the dirt, and put the mint in the new dirt, roots first. I added more dirt on top then watered the pots. I placed them where they could get plenty of sun for growth.

God wants us to be rooted in Him so we can grow. Sometimes in order to be rooted, He separates us from our comfortable place to unfamiliar territory. The feeling of moving to unfamiliar territory can sometimes feel like a burden or being buried.

If you feel like you're buried with burdens, now is not the time to do nothing. Water yourself and aim toward the Son, Jesus, to helyyp you grow. Pretty soon you will outgrow that place and come out of being planted in one spot. You will multiply and produce beautiful things.

The process of growing from being planted is not easy. It might seem like it's taking forever to produce. Don't worry about how long it takes, don't stop watering you because if you do, you will dry up and won't be able to produce anything. If you dry up, you will have to start the process all over again.

In the Bible, a man named Jacob left is hometown to go on a journey to find a wife. He was doing this to obey his father. While he was a sleep on the journey God spoke to him in Genesis 28: 15, *"I am with you and will watch over you wherever you go, and I will bring you back to this land. I will not leave you until I have done what I have promised you."*

Jacob didn't get the promise from God until he obeyed. He took the first step toward what he was supposed to do by leaving his comfort zone. God met Jacob on the journey and told him He was with him.

I encourage you to take the step toward being rooted in God. It will help you to maintain peace and joy. Changing your lifestyle might feel like you're buried at first, but you are planted to grow deep roots in God. Getting planted might feel uncomfortable, but God will be with you every step of the way.

DAY 15: Planted

Questions

1. Do you feel like you are being planted now?
2. What steps have taken or are going to take to start growing?

_____
_____
_____
_____
_____
_____
_____
_____
_____
_____
_____
_____
_____
_____
_____
_____
_____
_____
_____
_____
_____

DAY 15: Planted

Prayer

Dear Lord,

Thank you for all you have done. I thank you for the time of being planted so that I can be rooted in you. Please keep me at peace and help me to not worry about tomorrow. Please guide me in this stage of growth so that I can produce good things that bring you glory.

In Jesus name. Amen.

_____

_____

_____

_____

_____

_____

_____

_____

_____

_____

_____

_____

_____

_____

_____

_____

_____

_____

DAY 16: The Words You Speak

Proverbs 21:23 says, *"He who guards his mouth and his tongue, guards his soul from troubles."*

God didn't create the world by chiseling everything with a hammer and knife; He spoke it into existence. Jesus spoke power, healing and love. His miracles didn't always require Him to touch someone, sometimes he just spoke and it was done.

A Biblical example is the man who was by the pool who needed healing, Jesus told him to pick up your bed and walk. The man didn't have to get into the pool nor did Jesus touch Him physically, it took words and faith.

John 5:8-9 *"Then Jesus said to him, "Get up! Pick up your mat and walk." At once the man was cured; he picked up his mat and walked."*

Speaking over yourself is so powerful. You can speak things into existence over your life. This is not to be done in a manipulative way, but in a faith way.

"Death and life are in the power of the tongue, and those who love it will eat its fruit" Proverbs 18:21.

Words are the water that's needed when we are planted. Water helps the seeds to grow by germinating them. Germination is the beginning of the growth for the seeds after a period of dormancy. (12) If the seed is not watered, it's not coming out of being dormant.

After watering the seed there is still a process must happen for the seed to grow. It actually has to be watered often so that proper nutrients needed for growth gets through the dirt, to the seed.

Watering yourself and others, with positive words takes time. It must be consistent so that the words can get through all of the dirt in your mind. It's good to wake with a positive attitude, pray, and go about the day. A person that is constantly watering themselves with positive words, never seems to have a bad day even if they did. Someone that doesn't water themselves enough, their thoughts take a negative turn. The dirt dries out and no nutrients is getting through to the mind. This is what Proverbs 18:21 means. If you keep watering yourself then eventually something will come up out of the dirt. The words that you have been watering yourself with will be either something healthy and beautiful, or unhealthy and brown.

When plants have dead leaves, or when a whole plant die, either it has to be pruned or the plant has to be thrown away. Negative words can cause the growth in your life to stop the growing process. Then the process of being planted will have to start over again.

Proverbs 12:25 *"Anxiety weighs down the heart, but a kind word cheers it up."*

Words have the power to heal. Words have the power to remove anxiety and depression. Therapist are doctors that use words to heal.

Use your words to heal your broken heart. Use your words to help heal others. The Bible gives promises and is a guide on how to use words for healing. For example, if you are having an insecure moment about doing a task at work, remember you are more than conqueror like it says in Romans 8:37. Repeat that to yourself until the water gets down in the seed and your attitude about the task changes.

Rejuvenate your spirit with your words.

DAY 16: The Words You Speak

Questions

1. Write down positive things about yourself.
2. How did the positive things make you feel?

_____

_____

_____

_____

_____

_____

_____

_____

_____

_____

_____

_____

_____

_____

_____

_____

_____

_____

_____

_____

_____

_____

_____

_____

_____

DAY 16: The Words You Speak

Prayer

Dear Lord,

Thank you for giving me a voice to speak. Thank you for the Bible. Please give me the mind to remember to water myself, and others, with positive words. Lord, I ask that you water me with your words and that your words be the loudest in my mind so that I can be rooted in you.

In Jesus name. Amen.

_____

_____

_____

_____

_____

_____

_____

_____

_____

_____

_____

_____

_____

_____

_____

_____

DAY 17: It's Time to Obey God

Obeying God is important to rejuvenating our spirits. Obey: comply with the command, direction, or request of authority. (13)

Obedience: compliance with an order, request, or law or submission to another's authority. (14)

Remember we are not saved through obeying God, we are saved through salvation. We are saved because we believe Jesus is God's son, He rose on the third day, and He sits in heaven with God. We are saved because we confess that we were sinners.

Obedience shows God that we love and trust Him. John 14:23 says, *"Jesus replied, "Anyone who loves me will obey my teaching. My Father will love them, and we will come to them and make our home with them. 24 Anyone who does not love me will not obey my teaching. These words you hear are not my own; they belong to the Father who sent me."*

Jesus tells this to the disciples when He is explaining that He is going to leave them with the Holy Spirit. Jesus says "if you love me, keep my commands" three times in this passage. Two times after He says it He follows with "my Father will love them."

This maybe confusing because God loves everyone. The Bible says so in John 3:16. When we love God back, He can be with us always. When we live a life pleasing to God, He will never leave us.

Let's go back to the plant metaphor. Plants also need light to grow and be their best selves. The mint that I have outside is leaning toward the direction of the sun. When I look at the mint, I know which direction the sun hits them the most. The plants need sun because it gives them energy. The sun and water combined allows the plants to breath and live. If either one of these elements are missing, the plant will not survive and have to be uprooted, then replanted again.

The sun is obedience, God's word is the water. Obedience and God's word go together to help us to continue to live. Blessings come when we obey God and not our own desires.

"Do not merely listen to the word, and so deceive yourselves. Do what it says. Anyone who listens to the word but does not do what it says is like someone who looks at his face in a mirror and, after looking at himself, goes away and immediately forgets what he looks like. But whoever looks intently into the perfect law that gives freedom, and continues in it—not forgetting what they have heard, but doing it—they will be blessed in what they do." James 1:22-25

DAY 17: It's Time to Obey God

Questions

1. Is God telling you to do something regarding your life that you haven't done?
2. If the answer is yes, write out your thoughts. If the answer is no, write out thoughts about obeying God more.

_____

_____

_____

_____

_____

_____

_____

_____

_____

_____

_____

_____

_____

_____

_____

_____

_____

_____

_____

_____

DAY 17: It's Time to Obey God

Prayer

Dear Lord,

Thank you for your Word and love. Thank you for opening my eyes to areas in my life that I need to obey you in. Please give me the strength to obey you. I struggle in this area (name the area), and it's hard for me to obey you when it comes to this. Thank you for your grace and mercy.

In Jesus name. Amen.

_____
_____
_____
_____
_____
_____
_____
_____
_____
_____
_____
_____
_____
_____
_____
_____
_____

DAY 18: Pray and Fast

Throughout the Bible, there are many examples of praying and fasting when a move of God was needed. The move of God isn't a financial blessing, but it is believing God will move upon the hearts of people. A move of God is also needed for us to be delivered spiritually. A move of God is also needed for others to believe.

Jesus told His disciples when they failed at casting out a demonic spirit, *"But this kind does not go out except through fasting and praying."* Matthew 17:21 NKJV.

In Matthew 17:20 is the "faith the size of a mustard seed can move mountains" scripture. In order to receive the faith needed to move mountains, prayer and fasting has to be done.

Isaiah 58 explains the importance of fasting. Paraphrase, fasting is away to break strongholds from ourselves, to strengthen us, and the spirit of the Lord will be upon us so that we can break strongholds from others. Fasting is an act of love for yourself and others, therefore God honors fasting.

Fasting 40 days and 40 nights like Jesus did is overwhelming. Start off small, maybe fast one meal per day. Spend the time in prayer, worshipping God, and reading the Bible, instead of eating. Let God lead you in your prayer and fasting life. He will give you direction on what to do.

Praying brings peace to our minds. When we give everything to God, we put it in His hands to handle the things on our minds that bring us anxiety. Philippians 4:4-7 sums up why we should pray and how we should pray.

"Rejoice in the Lord always. I will say it again: Rejoice! Let your gentleness be evident to all. The Lord is near. Do not be anxious about anything, but in every situation, by prayer and petition, with thanksgiving, present your requests to God. And the peace of God, which transcends all understanding, will guard your hearts and your minds in Christ Jesus."

Prayer is like calling your best friend on the phone when something crazy happened, and the anxious feeling of 'I just need to talk to someone to get it out of off my chest' happens. After you talk to someone, a feeling of relief comes over you. You spoke what was on your mind into the atmosphere. By speaking your concerns, you transferred your feelings unto another person. This is why it is important to discern relationships. Everyone will not receive your problems and victories with the correct mindset. Also, you can't let everyone vent to you because you might be having a fantastic day then your best friend calls with all of her problems. After the phone conversation you might start feeling anxious the same way she did, but you don't know why. The anxious feeling is on you because you took on their emotions when they vented to you, this is called transfer of spirits.

There is someone that will always receive everything you speak to Him correctly, and His name is Jesus. He will take your problems and give you peace every time you confide in Him.

Instead of questions for today, write out your prayer requests. There is extra space for today.

DAY 18: Pray and Fast

Prayer Request

_____

_____

_____

_____

_____

_____

_____

_____

_____

_____

_____

_____

_____

DAY 18: Pray and Fast

Prayer

Dear Lord,

Thank you for all you have done for us. Thank you for salvation. I come to you with all of my prayer request. I'm laying them down at your feet. I thank you for what you are going to do with my request. I thank you for the peace that you have given me. The peace comes from you because I have faith that you are God and you are in control.

In Jesus name. Amen.

_____

_____

_____

_____

_____

_____

_____

_____

_____

_____

_____

_____

_____

_____

_____

_____

DAY 19: Delight in God

"Keep God First" sounds like a cliché but it truly is the answer to everything. God is the answer to finding purpose. He's the answer to the direction for our lives.

"Take delight in the LORD, and he will give you the desires of your heart." Psalm 37:4

Delight in this scripture means to take pleasure in and enjoyment. God is supposed to be our pleasure and enjoyment, not the things of the world. We should always turn to God first when problems arise that we can't handle. We also should always turn to God first when everything is going great.

By delighting in the Lord, seeking His presence, and aligning our desires with His will, we can experience a deep connection with Him. As a result, God promises to grant the desires of our hearts, which are shaped by a close walk with Him. Our desires will transform to His desires.

Remember God's desires? He desires are for us to have an abundant life, to love Him first, and love ourselves so that we can love others.

As we delight in God, we will delight and love ourselves more. Our love for others will grow more. Most importantly, our love for God will grow more.

Delighting in God will eventually change our behavior because of the love we will develop for God and ourselves. For example, a healthier lifestyle might develop, a career change, becoming more organized, and getting rid of bad habits and addictions. A desire to have a more positive outlook on life will occur, as well as an overall peace of mind.

"For I know the plans I have for you," declares the LORD, "plans to prosper you and not to harm you, plans to give you hope and a future. Then you will call on me and come and pray to me, and I will listen to you. You will seek me and find me when you seek me with all your heart." Jeremiah 29:11-13.

God has great plans to prosper us. These plans will manifest the more we seek Him wholeheartedly. The seeking God has to be done because we love Him. We all desire real love and to not be used by people. Therefore, we shouldn't seek God because we need something, we should seek Him because we love Him.

DAY 19: Delight in God

Questions

1. Why should you delight in God?
2. How can delighting in God change your life?

_____
_____
_____
_____
_____
_____
_____
_____
_____
_____
_____
_____
_____
_____
_____
_____
_____
_____
_____
_____
_____
_____
_____
_____
_____
_____

DAY 19: Delight in God

Prayer

Dear Lord,

Thank you for allow us, the opportunity to seek you. Thank you for the Bible, thank you for the Holy Spirit. Allow us to see you in our everyday lives. Allow us to see you in our surroundings. Help us to recognize when you are speaking to us. Keep us near you so that we will not stray from seeking you.

In Jesus name. Amen.

_____
_____
_____
_____
_____
_____
_____
_____
_____
_____
_____
_____
_____
_____
_____
_____

DAY 20: The Battle is Won

I love sports. I like football, basketball, soccer, and track are my favorites. I enjoy all of the Olympic games also. I like the competition and the battle to determine the winner. Occasionally, the winner of the game can be determined before the game starts. The winning team can be determined because of the record of games (stats) the team has one, by the players, and the coaches.

Wouldn't it be nice to know the outcome of everything you are battling against in life? I have some good news. The winner has been determined. The winner is you with God on your side.

1 Corinthians 15:57 says, *"But thanks be to God! He gives us the victory through our Lord Jesus Christ."*

We have victory through Jesus. When He died on the cross, then rose again, Jesus died for our sins so that we can be saved. Sins includes, healing physically, mentally, and spiritually.

Isaiah 53:5 says, *"But He was wounded for our transgressions, He was [b]bruised for our iniquities; The chastisement for our peace was upon Him, And by His stripes[c] we are healed."*

Jesus died on the cross for our healing in every area of our lives. We would live in a perfect world, but the devil, also known as Satan is just as real as God. The devil wants to rule the world by convincing us to do what he says instead of God. He wants us to make other things our god so that he will win the spiritual war.

Ephesians 6:12 says, *" For we do not wrestle against flesh and blood, but against principalities, against powers, against the rulers of [a]the darkness of this age, against spiritual hosts of wickedness in the heavenly places. "*

This ongoing war is why bad things keep happening in the world. Sometimes it feels like everything in life goes wrong all at once, but we can't give in to changing sides during these times. We have to remain on God's side because He is the one that wants us to prosper abundantly in every area of our lives.

We stay on God's side by always looking out for the devil. We have to be aware of when we are going over to the wrong side. We have to guard our hearts and minds like a soldier protecting a precious jewel.

The Bible tells us how to stand guard.

Ephesians 6: 10-11 says, *"Finally, my brethren, be strong in the Lord and in the power of His might. 11 Put on the whole armor of God, that you may be able to stand against the [b]wiles of the devil.*

Ephesians 6:14-18 says, *"Stand firm then, with the belt of truth buckled around your waist, with the breastplate of righteousness in place, and with your feet fitted with the readiness that comes from the gospel of peace. In addition to all this, take up the shield of faith, with which you can extinguish all the flaming arrows of the evil one. Take the helmet of salvation and the sword of the Spirit, which is the word of God. And pray in the Spirit on all occasions with all kinds of prayers and requests. With this in mind, be alert and always keep on praying for all the Lord's people.*

This passage of scripture is using a suite of armor as a metaphor for how we should stay on guard against the devil. The summarization of the passage is we should keep doing right and stay peaceful. We should keep the faith of believing in God. We should read the Word of God, the Bible, and always pray. Doing all of these things diligently will rejuvenate our spirts and prevent them from being empty again. It is possible to live a life always on full of hope and joy, no matter what is going on around us.

DAY 20: The Battle is Won

Questions

1. What are the ways we can stand against the devil?
2. What battles in your life is God fighting for you now?

_____

_____

_____

_____

_____

_____

_____

_____

_____

_____

_____

_____

_____

_____

_____

_____

_____

_____

_____

_____

_____

DAY 20: The Battle is Won

Prayer

Dear Lord,

Thank you so much for winning the ultimate battle of dying on the cross and rising from the grave. I face many things that I need you to fight for me Lord. I know that you have the victory over the devil. I believe that you want me to prosper abundantly in every area of my life. I lay down all of the things bothering me at your feet. Thank you God for handling these things for me.

In Jesus name, Amen.

_____

_____

_____

_____

_____

_____

_____

_____

_____

_____

_____

_____

_____

DAY 21: Beauty for Ashes

Life often presents us with trials and tribulations that leave us feeling broken and defeated, much like ashes from a fire. Fortunately, with God we have the capacity to rise from the ashes and embrace transformation. This journey of renewal and restoration is beautifully depicted throughout the Bible. Through scriptures we are led on this journey to end at hope and healing.

"and provide for those who grieve in Zion— to bestow on them a crown of beauty instead of ashes, the oil of joy instead of mourning, and a garment of praise instead of a spirit of despair.
They will be called oaks of righteousness, a planting of the LORD for the display of his splendor."
Isaiah 61:3

This scripture speaks of God's desire to replace the ashes of sorrow and mourning with a crown of beauty, joy, and praise. God wants to turn our pain into purpose and trials into victory.

There is another scripture that speaks of God transforming sadness into joy. It is Psalms 30:11-12.

"You turned my wailing into dancing; you removed my sackcloth and clothed me with joy, that my heart may sing your praises and not be silent. LORD my God, I will praise you forever."

A sackcloth was a sign of grief, mourning, or sadness that was actually worn so that others new those in mourning. God removes the sackcloth and clothes us with joy. He gives us hope even during tough times.

I hope that this journal helped to rejuvenate your spirit. Trials and tribulations will always exist but never lose sight on God's desires for your life. God always works everything out for those that seek Him first.

Romans 8:28 says, *"And we know that in all things God works for the good of those who love him, who[a] have been called according to his purpose."*

DAY 21: Beauty for Ashes

Questions

1. How has this journal helped you?

_____

_____

_____

_____

_____

_____

_____

_____

_____

_____

_____

_____

_____

_____

_____

_____

_____

_____

_____

_____

_____

_____

_____

DAY 21: Beauty for Ashes

My Prayer for Everyone

Dear Lord,

Thank you for every person going through this journey. I pray that you will touch each one with your love. I pray that they will be rejuvenated, filled with peace and joy. I pray that you will give them the strength to walk into their purpose and your will for their lives. I pray for those that don't know you as their Savior, I pray that their souls will be saved when they confess they believe that Jesus is God's son. I pray everyone's spirit will be eternally rejuvenated.

In Jesus name. Amen.

_____

_____

_____

_____

_____

_____

_____

_____

_____

_____

_____

_____

_____

Journaling Pages

References

HarperCollins Christian Publishing, Inc. June 28, 2023. *Bible Gateway.* All Scriptures NKJV and NIV <www.biblegateway.com>

Oxford English Dictionary. 2023. *Oxford English Dictionary.* All definitions 1-14. <www.oed.com>

Cover credit: Designed by Talisa Lauray through Typorama app

.

Made in the USA
Columbia, SC
11 August 2024

39818113R00065